BIG STUFF IN THE MARITIMES

BOOK # 1

Katherine E. Tapley-Milton

PUBLISHED BY

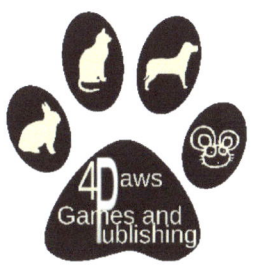

BRUNO, SASKATCHEWAN, CANADA

Big Stuff in the Maritimes, Book # 1

Written and Created by Katherine E. Tapley-Milton

Photos by Katherine E. Tapley-Milton

"The Dill" photo courtesy of Scott Smith

Cover Art by 4 Paws Games and Publishing

Cover Photo Edited by Athena Whitbread

Edited by Kathrine E. Tapley-Milton and 4 Paws Games and Publishing

Formatted and Published by 4 Paws Games and Publishing
Published January 2017 First Edition
ISBN 13: 978-1-988345-39-0
Copyright © 2017 by Katherine E. Tapley-Milton
All Rights Reserved
Published by 4 Paws Games and Publishing
P.O. Box 444
Humboldt, Saskatchewan, Canada S0K 2A0
http://www.4-Paws-Games-and-Publishing.ca
Publishing logo and name copyright © 2016
All Rights Reserved

The publisher is not responsible for the book, website, or social media (or its content) that is not owned by the publisher. All legal matters are to be taken up by the author as the publisher holds no responsibilities.

The author and publisher have made every effort to ensure the accuracy of the information within this book was correct at time of publication. The author and publisher acknowledge that not every location is in the book at this time.

No part of this publication may be reproduced, distributed, or transmitted in any form or by any means, including photocopying, recording, or other electronic or mechanical methods, without the prior written permission of the publisher, except in the case of brief quotations embodied in critical reviews and certain other non-commercial uses permitted by copyright law.

Attention: Permission C/O
Katherine E. Tapley-Milton
18 Squire Street
Sackville, New Brunswick E4L 4K9

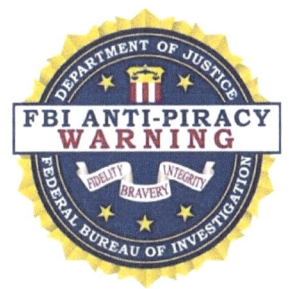

Other Books by Katherine E. Tapley-Milton

Big Stuff in the Maritimes Series
1-3

Other Books
Kathy's Down East Christmas Cookbook
Mother Tapley's Recipe Book: Tasty Down East Cooking
The Disappearing Mailboxes of New Brunswick and Nova Scotia: A Touring of Mailboxes
Old Boats and Old Quotes
The Adventures of the Three Mouse-Breath-Kateers
The Adventures of Sir Lancelot the Cat
Scintillating Scarecrows
And more.

Find Katherine Online
Website
http://authorkatherinetapleymilton.weebly.com

Facebook
https://www.facebook.com/KatherineETapleyMilton

Amazon Authors Central Page
https://www.amazon.com/Katherine-Tapley-Milton/e/B00CP8EBR8

Like the book? Please post a review online where you bought it!

TABLE OF CONTENTS

Preface 1
Acknowledgements 3
Introduction 4
New Brunswick 6
   Aulac 6
      Semipalmated Sandpipers 7
   Blackville 8
      Salmon Fly 9
   Campbellton 10
      Restigouche Sam 11
   Caraquet 12
      The Giant Conch Shell 13
   Doaktown 14
      Bruce the Moose 15
   Kedgwick 16
      The Lumberjack 17
   Magnetic Hill 18
      The Magnet 19
   Maugerville 20
      Giant Potato 21
   Nackawic 22
   Plaster Rock 24

- White-Tailed Deer 25
- Sackville 26
  - The Semipalmated Sanderling Sandpiper Carving 27
- Salisbury 28
  - The Silver Fox 29
- Shediac 30
  - The Big Lobster 31
- Sussex 32
  - Daisy and Buttercup 33
- Nova Scotia 34
  - Auld's Cove 34
    - The Mariner 35
  - Berwick 36
    - The Berwick Apple 37
  - Oxford 38
    - The Giant Blueberry 39
  - Stewiacke 40
    - Polar Bear 41
  - St. Peters 42
    - Glad Tidings Toy Soldiers 43
  - Truro 44
    - Truro Glooscap 45
  - Windsor 46

The Howard Dill Statue	47
Prince Edward Island	48
Cavendish	48
Bear Made of Nails	49
Cavendish	50
Giant Lobster	51
Summerside	52
Starlite Ice Cream	53
Poem on Big Stuff	54
About Katherine E. Tapley-Milton	56

PREFACE

I have been working on "Big Stuff in the Maritimes" for many years now. Every time we took a vacation in the Maritimes, I was delighted to photograph some folk-art statues, just for fun and my own personal use. There have been many magazine articles done on some of the statues, but there aren't any books specifically for the Maritime provinces. I used "Large Canadian Roadside Attractions"[1] in my research. However, I mainly utilized lists found in: "Big Things in Nova Scotia"[2]; "Big Things in New Brunswick"[3]; and "Big Things in Prince Edward Island"[4] as maps for my photography. I also consulted the following list of statues that were extremely helpful:

http://www.bigthings.ca/bignb.html

http://www.bigthings.ca/bigns.html; and http://www.bigthings.ca/bigpei.html.

Finally, I could not have done this book without the help of my husband, Dave, who drove me around and did some backup photos for me. He is an indispensable part of this book.

---

[1] http://roadsideattractions.ca/

[2] http://roadsideattractions.ca/novascotia.html

[3] http://roadsideattractions.ca/newbrunswick.html

[4] http://www.bigthings.ca/bigpei.html

In the process of photographing and researching, "Big Stuff in the Maritimes", I came to know the Maritime provinces much better and learned a lot of history as well.

ACKNOWLEDGEMENTS

    I would like to dedicate this book to my husband, Dave Milton, who assisted me with driving, photography, and his patient listening to my plans for "Big Stuff in the Maritimes."

I like the following quote about inspiration in writing:

"It's the witching hour once more-

When the Muse comes out to play.

He calls me through that magic door-

Where galaxies of worlds await!"

—Belle Whittington

INTRODUCTION

Dotting the landscape of Prince Edward Island, New Brunswick, and Nova Scotia are wonderful folk-art statues. These statues are often symbolic of what the areas are famous for. For example, the large lobster in Shediac, New Brunswick trumpets the fact that this town is the lobster capital of the world. Then there is the sizeable blueberry in Oxford, Nova Scotia that shows everyone this town is famous for its blueberry industry. The big potato in Maugerville, New Brunswick is part of a vegetable farm where potatoes are grown. Then there is Daisy and Buttercup, the statue of a cow and calf in Sussex, New Brunswick that symbolizes their dairy industry. Of course, in Prince Edward Island, there is a large statue of a cow to advertise Cows Ice cream.

Will Ferguson gives an instructive quote about folk-art statues:

"Large objects have a definite, tongue-in-cheek cachet, and there is a surprising amount of local pride invested in them ... High ideals of democratic folk art and totemistic effigies aside,

Canada's roadside attractions are the national equivalent of garden gnomes."[5]

      My husband and I traveled throughout the Maritimes shooting the pictures of folk-art statues that are in this book. We had a lot of fun doing it, and it was very educational. We generally avoided the statues in inner cities because there are too many of them, and they are not classified as folk art. Some of the statues in this book are chainsaw art, fiberglass, concrete, metals, etc. We used a child's pink tricycle in each statue photo to give the reader an idea of how big the statues are.

      It is our hope that this book series, "Big Stuff in the Maritimes," will inspire tourists and native Maritimers alike to go off the beaten track and find some of these statues while discovering whole new parts of the Maritimes. If you do, you will be delighted with giant salmons, fiddles, lumberjacks, moose, and many fantastical forms. Maybe you can plan your next vacation hunting for the big stuff in the Maritimes.

---

[5] http://www.willferguson.ca/articles/sizematters.html

NEW BRUNSWICK
AULAC

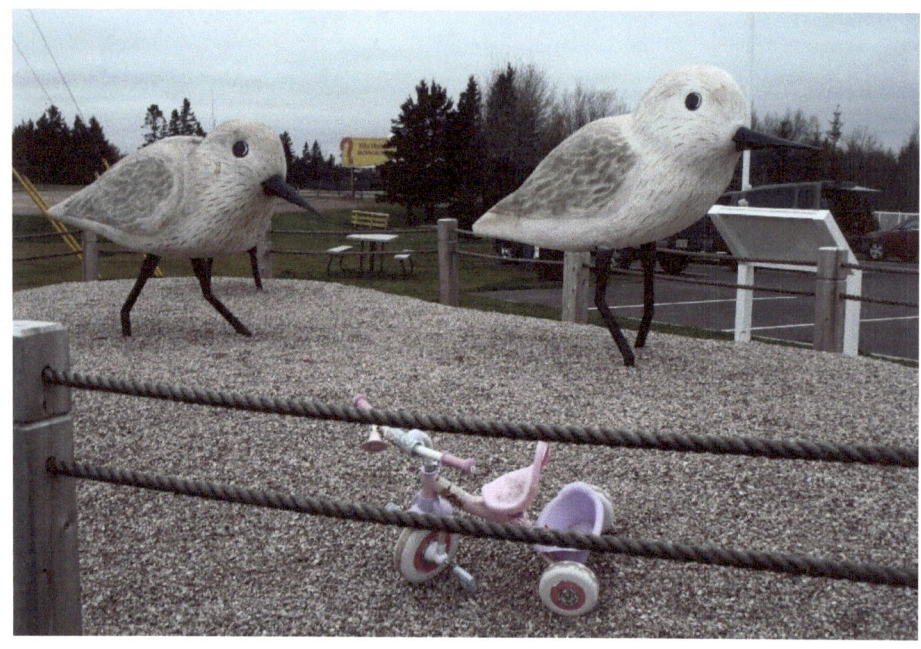

SEMIPALMATED SANDPIPERS

A new edition to the grounds of the Aulac Big Stop in New Brunswick is a bunch of Semipalmated Sandpiper statues, which are fenced in by rope. In an article titled, "People and Peeps" by Dr. Ladybug it explains that, *"More than two million shorebirds stop each year in the upper Bay of Fundy, in locations such as Johnson's Mills (and Dorchester Cape), to feed on the extensive intertidal mudflats during late summer en route to their wintering habitat in South America. Thirty-four species of shorebirds have been identified in the region; however, the Semipalmated Sandpiper, Calidris pusilla, far outnumbers the rest by making up as much as 95% of these massive flocks."*[6]

The mudflats in this region provide a steady supply of mud shrimp, which the Sandpipers like to feed on.

---

[6] https://www.geocaching.com/geocache/GC13Y4X_people-and-peepsguid=203fcf29-a7f5-4c52-b4f1-53cd9be65f19

BLACKVILLE

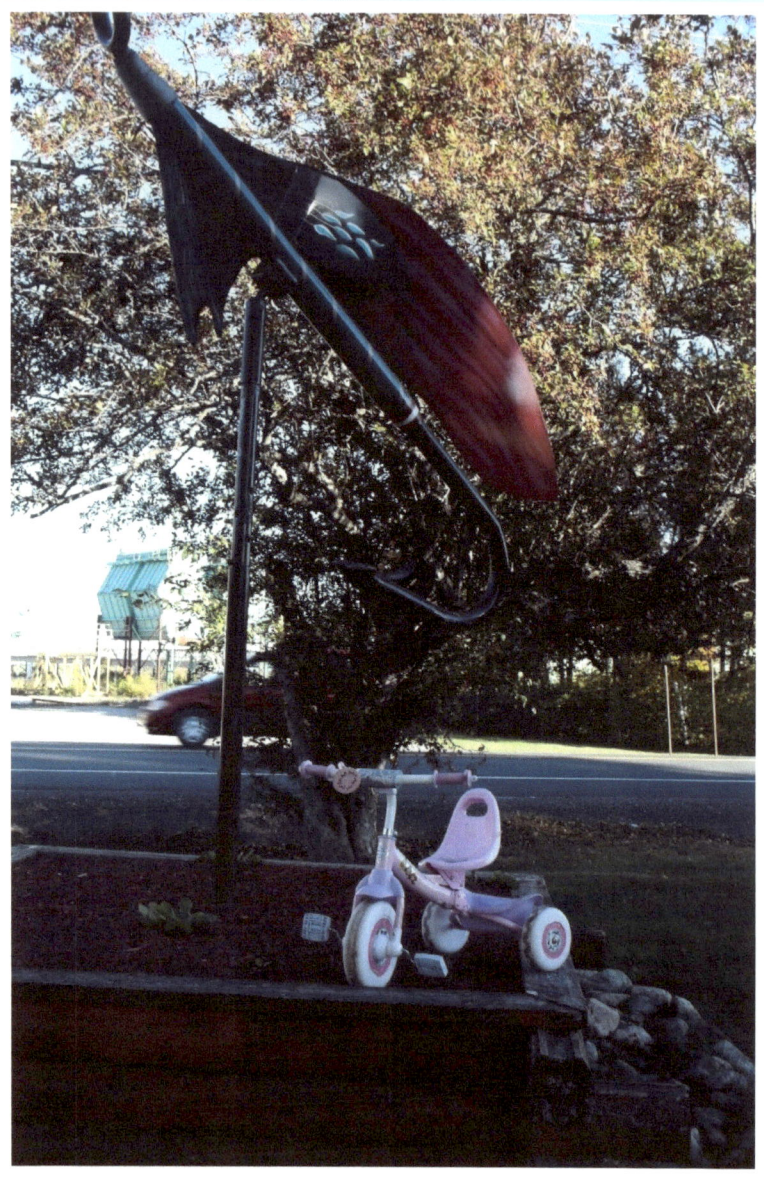

SALMON FLY

Blackville boasts that over 50% of North American salmon is caught in its Bartholomew and Miramichi Rivers. The village was incorporated in 1966 and has a population of 990.

It has a statue of the Dungarvon Whooper, and a giant salmon fly statue. Lumbering and fishing are Blackville's chief industries; however, tourism contributes to the economy as well. Blackville is on the southwest Miramichi River; 40 kilometers southwest of Miramichi...[7]

---

[7] https://en.wikipedia.org/wiki/Blackville,_New_Brunswick

CAMPBELLTON

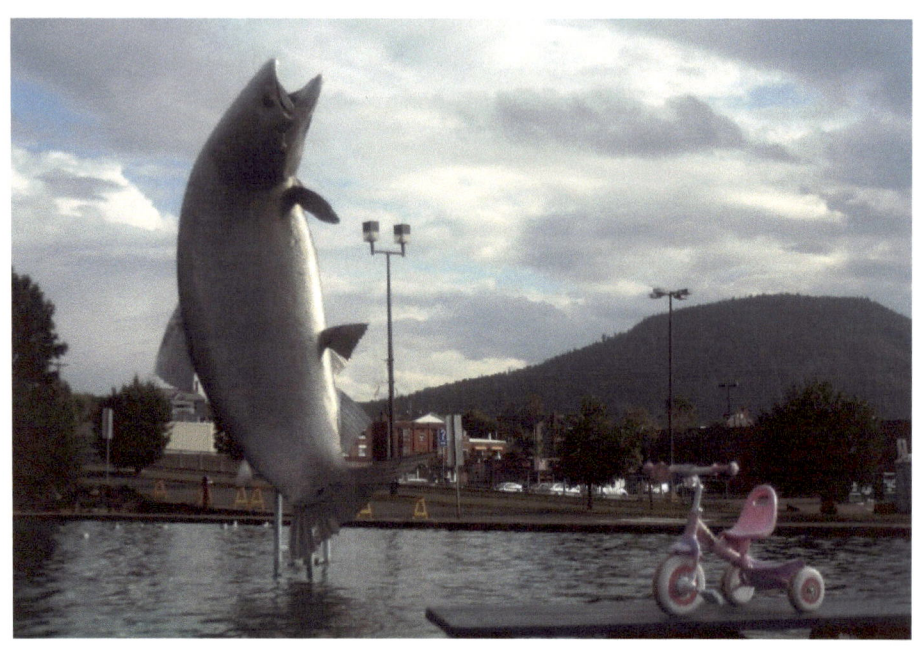

RESTIGOUCHE SAM

Campbellton, New Brunswick is well known for its wonderful salmon fishing, and in the middle of town, there is a fountain with a lively salmon statue jumping into the air. The salmon has a name. It is "Restigouche Sam." The statue stands 21.6 feet or 6.6 metres tall. It is built from, *"Approximately 2000 stainless steel scales, individually welded onto tubular steel, webbed in a superstructure. Approximately one ton of metal was used."*[8]

The builder of Restigouche Sam was William Lishman and Associates from Blackstock, Ontario.

Sam can be found in the Appalachian Range on Highway 11, in Restigouche County, New Brunswick. He is a dramatic and beautiful statue that gives the illusion of a real salmon jumping out of a river.

---

[8] https://www.bigthings.ca/newbruns/campbell.html

CARAQUET

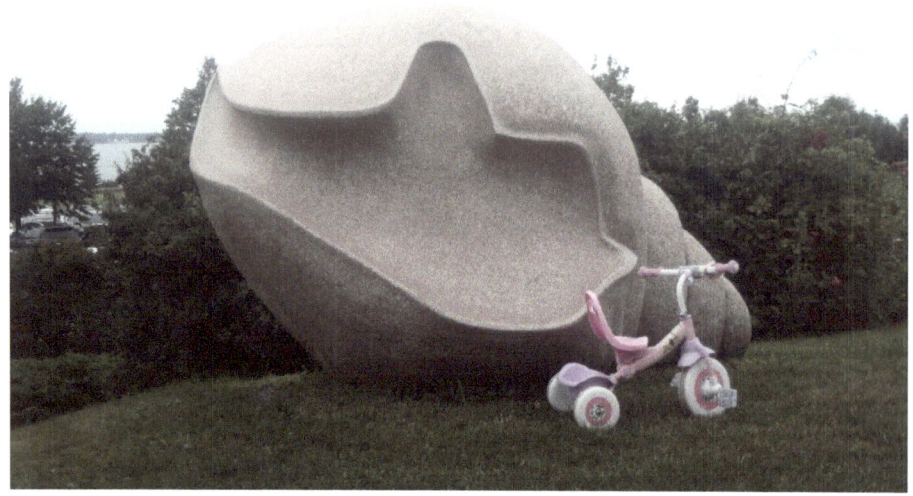

THE GIANT CONCH SHELL

Caraquet, New Brunswick is a small town on the Acadian Peninsular that has roughly, 4,000 people. It is in Gloucester County and boasts that it has the world's largest conch shell. This statue goes together with the world's largest clamshell which is close by. Atlantic Canada exports a lot of conch meat, which is, *"also known as rough or wave whelk, northern whelk, buckie, conchs coo coos ... (The) meat ranges from fresh (live) to whole cooked, frozen, pickled, smoked and canned."*[9]

Maritime sandbars are typically littered with conches, and around the world conches of various sizes and shapes are used in soups, stews, and chowders.

---

[9] http://atlanticcanadaexports.ca/product/whelk/

DOAKTOWN

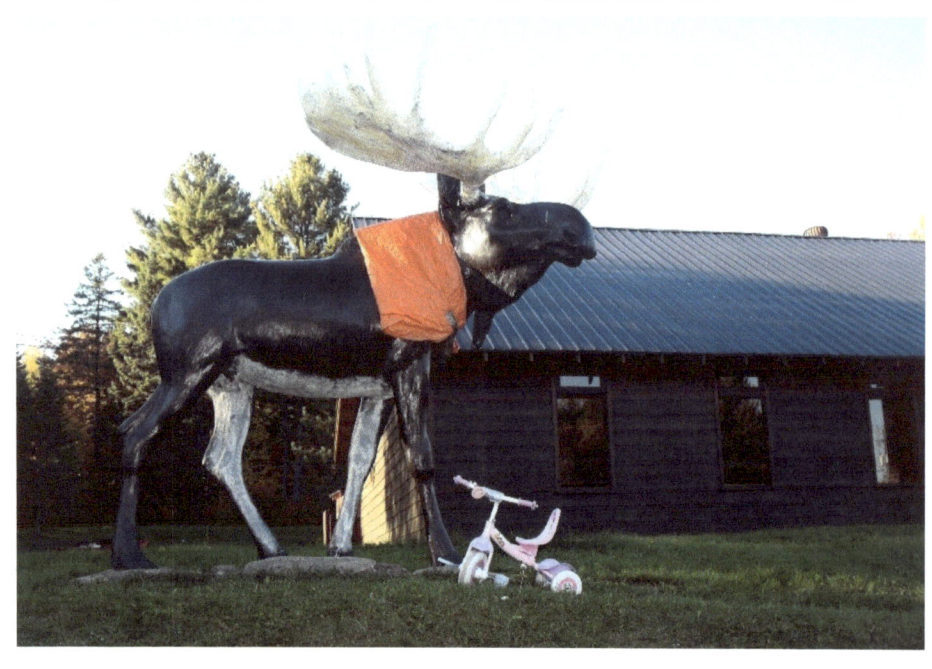

BRUCE THE MOOSE

Bruce the Moose is a life-sized replica of the real animal. A review of Taylor's Motel and Campground says, *"In the East end of the Village, on Highway 8, you will find 'Bruce the Moose' a life-sized statue 'guarding' the entrance to one of our finest restaurants. This attraction is beautifully landscaped ..."*[10]

The residents of Doaktown treat Bruce the Moose as an honored citizen. In the fall, Bruce must wear hunter orange or the radio station will call the restaurant and tell them to put it on him. They don't want Bruce to take a bullet.

---

[10] http://www.angelfire.com/biz/taylorsmotel/

KEDGWICK

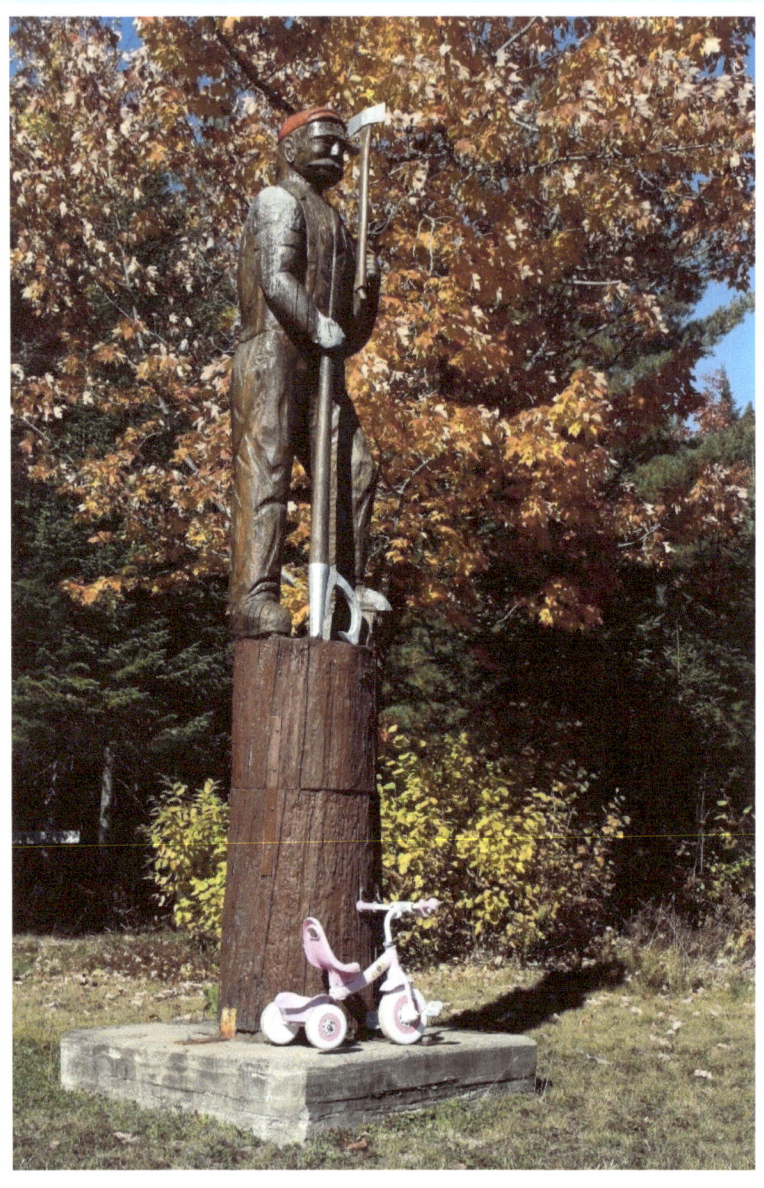

THE LUMBERJACK

In the village of Kedgwick, New Brunswick on Highway 17, stands a 25-foot (7.6 metre) tall lumberjack with an axe in one hand and a saw in the other. He is part of the Kedgwick Forestry Museum (Le Village et Musee Forestier de Kedgwick) and is called, "Ti-Nel". This Paul Bunyan of a statue was built in 1990 out of a big, red pine. The lumberjack's waist circumference is 8 feet (2.4 metres). He was designed by Conrad "Le Frere" Theriault.

According to The Canadian Encyclopedia©, *"The Village of Kedgwick is a Francophone community located 74 km southwest of Campbellton... Kedgwick was the site of many 19th-century lumber camps and was known then as Grande Fourche."*[11]

---

[11] http://www.thecanadianencyclopedia.ca/en/article/kedgwick/

MAGNETIC HILL

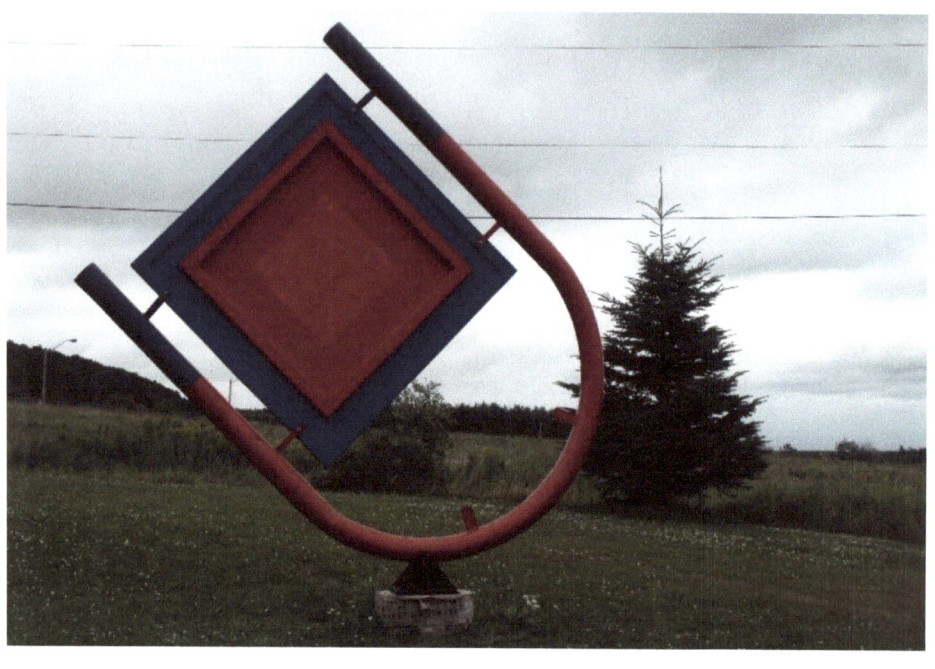

THE MAGNET

Magnetic Hill has both baffled and fascinated people since it was discovered in the nineteenth century. It is only now in the 21st century that a scientist believes he can explain the phenomenon. Kokichi Sugihara of Japan made a model in 2010 that he thinks replicates the mystery. He won a big award for his work. Kokichi explains the hill in terms of gravity and gradients, but urban legend says that aliens had a part in it.

Magnetic Hill's history is interesting; Wikipedia™ comments: *"Around 1931, it was noticed that at one point near the base of the ridge when driving south, motorists were required to accelerate to prevent rolling backward (i.e., what appears to be uphill)."*[12]

Eventually, this place was dubbed, "Magnetic Hill" and continues to fascinate tourists and locals alike. The curious come in vans, buses, motorbikes, cars, trucks, etc. To get to Magnetic Hill use Exit 450 and take Route 2 on the Trans-Canada Highway. The attraction is fifteen minutes from the center of Moncton, and incorporates a big zoo, gift shop and more.

---

[12] https://en.wikipedia.org/wiki/Magnetic_Hill_(Moncton

MAUGERVILLE

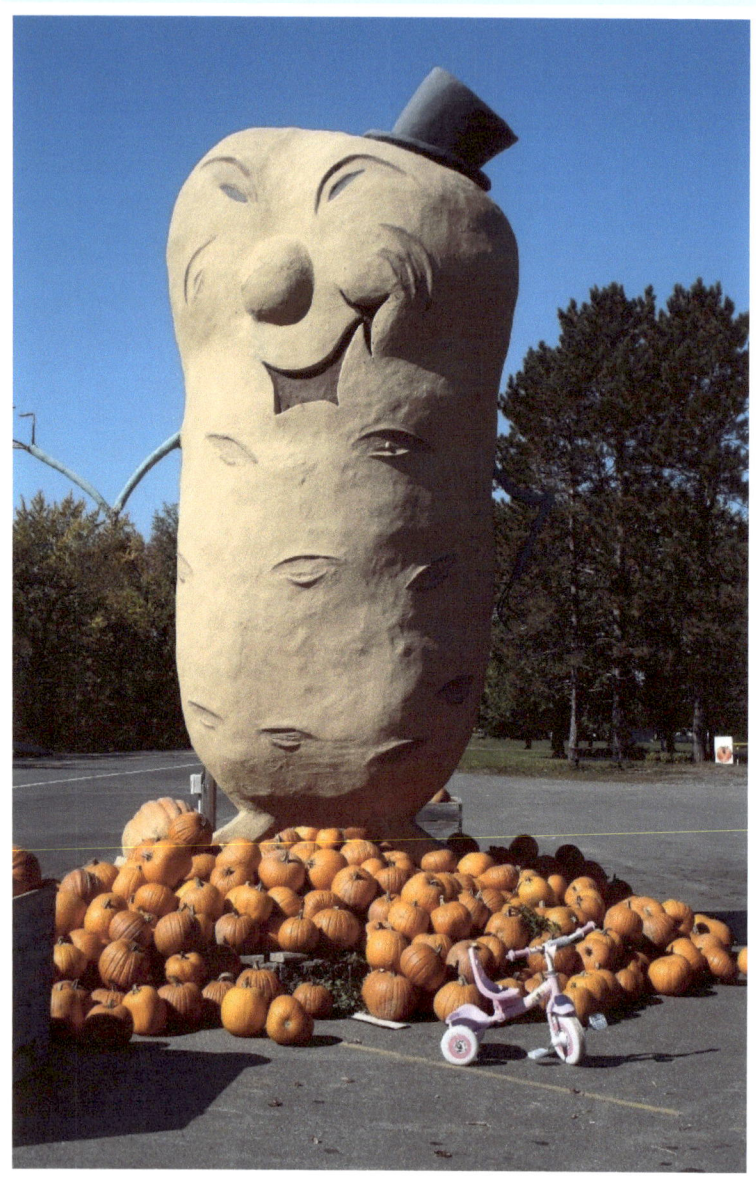

GIANT POTATO

One of the most outstanding landmarks in New Brunswick is Harvey's big potato. It was built in 1969. The spud's dimensions are 19 feet or 6 metres tall. It was constructed out of Ferro-cement. The big potato can be seen at Exit 312 of the Trans-Canada Highway near Fredericton. Why was it built? The giant statue is an advertising gimmick for Harvey's Vegetable Stand.

Henri Robideau, author of "Giant Canada", thinks that the towering tuber is a self-portrait. The starchy statue was built by Winston Bronnum, *"The late Winston Bronnum was a prolific artist who created some of the more impressive community monuments in Canada. So far, 6 have been identified. His studio was called Animaland and was located near the Timberline Motor Inn and Restaurant in Sussex, NB. He was largely self-taught and in his younger years worked on hydro dams and bridges, which apparently gave him insights that allowed him to create his large community monuments, which were primarily made of reinforced concrete. His carvings are in Canada Hall at Israel's Hebrew University and New York's Waldorf Hotel."*[13]

---

[13] http://www.bigthings.ca/artists/bronnum.html

NACKAWIC

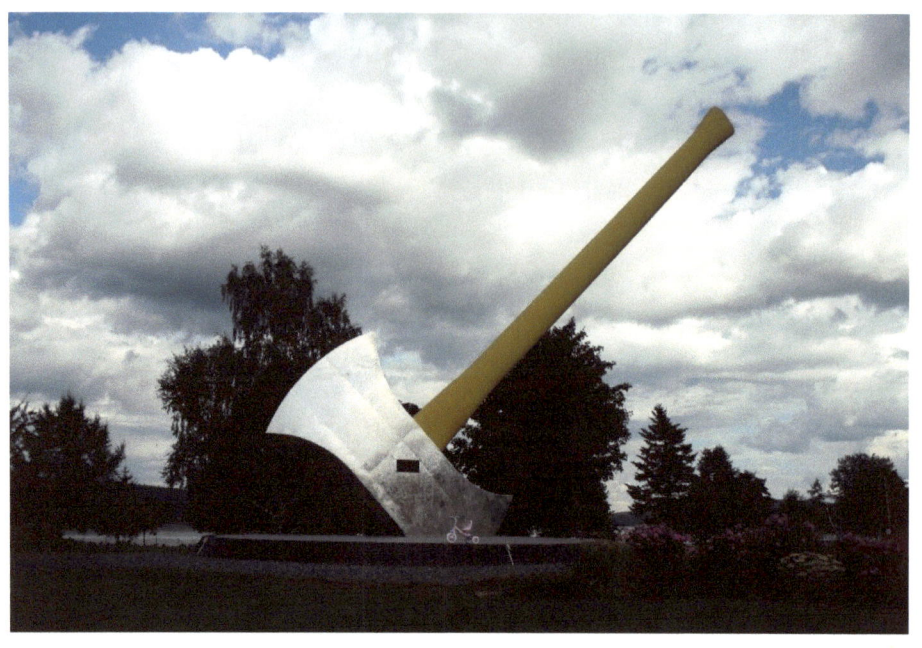

World's largest Axe

Nackawic, New Brunswick boasts that it has the world's largest axe. It is 15 meters or 49 feet tall and weighs fifty-five tons. The width is 7 meters or 23 feet, and the concrete base is 10 meters or 33 feet. Inside the head is a time capsule. The *Atlas Obscura* comments, *"Buried in the ground like the work of a frustrated giant, the World's Largest Axe is a monument to the importance of lumber and forestry and to the world's love of giant stuff. Built in 1991, the huge woodsman's tool is a gleaming symbol of the industrious lives and legacies of Canada's lumberjacks. In the same year, the axe was installed, its hometown was named the Forestry Capital of Canada, hence the colossal construction."*[14]

Although it was settled in the 1780s, it wasn't until 1960 that Nackawic came into existence. It was used to resettle farmers whose land was flooded by the Mactaquac Dam. A pulp and paper mill was built in the 1970s to provide work for those who lost their lands. The big axe is a favorite spot for tourists and impresses them with its sheer size.

---

[14] http://www.atlasobscura.com/places/world-s-largest-axe

PLASTER ROCK

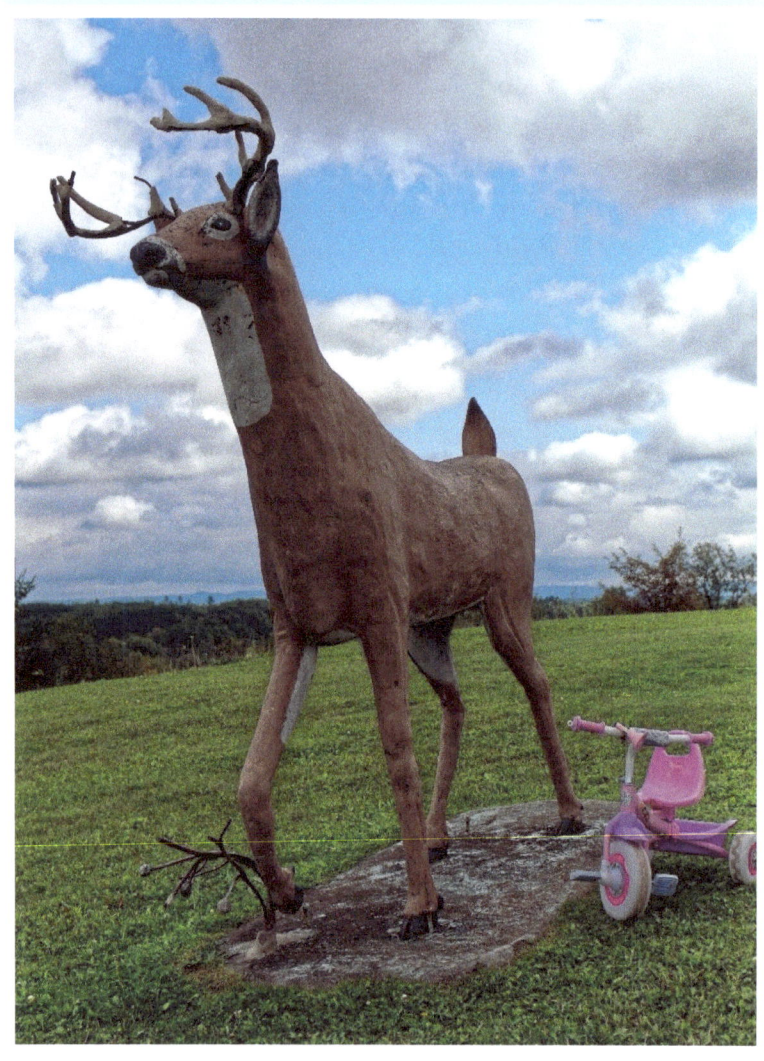

WHITE-TAILED DEER

Outside of the Irving Gas Station in Plaster Rock is the statue of a white-tailed deer that is very realistic. The first persons to settle Plaster Rock *"...were Hezekiah Day and his two brothers, who arrived in 1881. Plaster Rock was incorporated as the Village of Plaster Rock on November 9, 1966. Hezekiah Day gave Plaster Rock its name based on the hill on the other side of the Tobique River – the rock is made up of gypsum, or plaster."*[15]

Plaster Rock is a good place to hunt game and one hunter boasted that he shot a 339-pound buck there. There doesn't seem to be any information about the deer statue, but it symbolizes that the area has lots of game.

---

[15] http://plasterrockvillage.com/history/

SACKVILLE

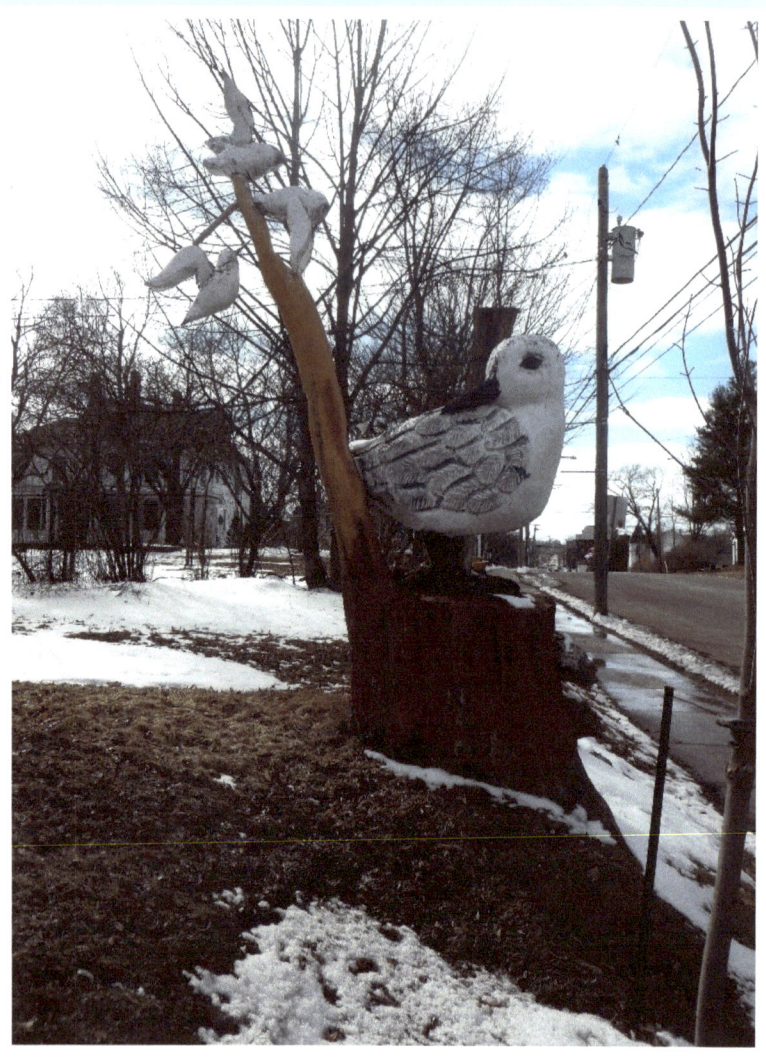

THE SEMIPALMATED SANDERLING SANDPIPER CARVING

On 59 Bridge Street in Sackville, New Brunswick there stands a large carving of a Semipalmated Sandpiper. Originally it was right outside *The Sanderling Bed and Breakfast*, which is no longer there. The man who carved this statue is Albert Deveau, who wore out three chain saws creating the sandpiper. Deveau hails from Edmundston, New Brunswick and used one whole elm tree for the giant bird. The sandpiper statue now stands on private property and can be readily seen by passersby.[16]

---

[16] https://sackville.com/wp-content/uploads/2016/01/sackvilleartswalk.pdf

SALISBURY

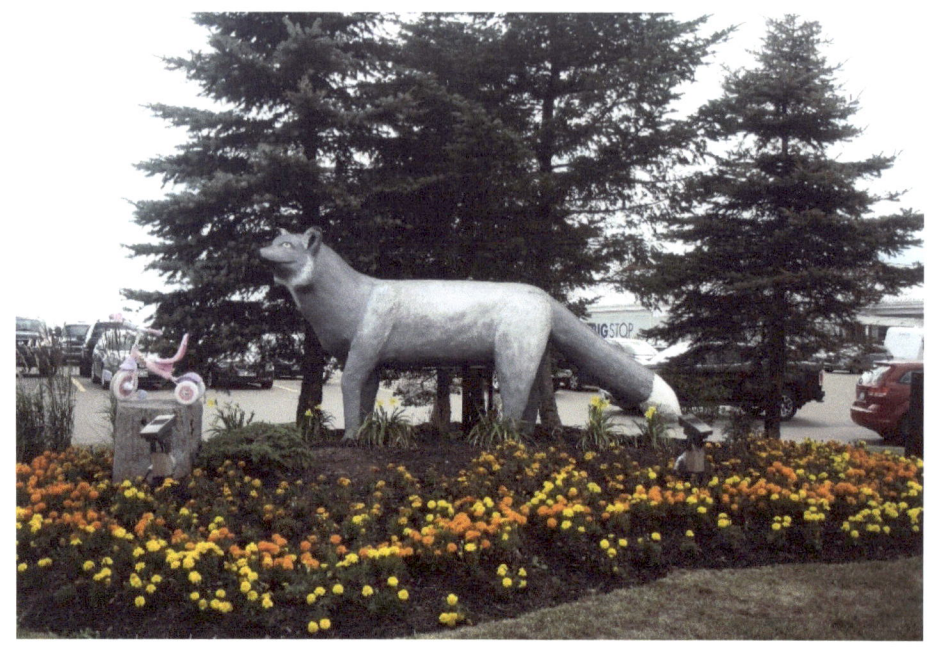

THE SILVER FOX

Salisbury, New Brunswick boasts "the world's largest silver fox" statue. Why? Tourism New Brunswick states: *"Salisbury was once a centre of Silver-fox ranching, and in tribute to that animal and the history of the industry, a commemorative statue of a larger-than-life, Silver fox can be seen today at the junction of the Trans-Canada Highway and Highway 112, at the Salisbury Irving service centre."*[17]

Before the Animal-Rights movement was in existence, fox farms started around 1910-1913 and were very profitable because everybody wanted real fur. The Salisbury area had the largest fox farms in the world. Colpitts Fox Ranch which had the largest fox farm in Canada was about 5 miles (8km) from the village. Now, all that is left is the wooden silver fox statue and artificial fox fur coats and stoles.

---

[17] http://www.tourismnewbrunswick.ca/Products/V/Village-of-Salisbury.aspx

SHEDIAC

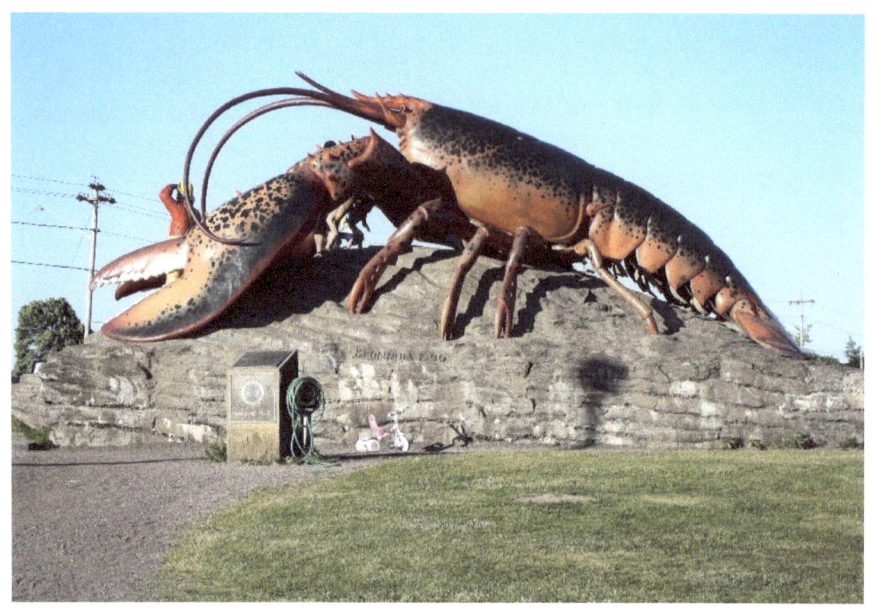

THE BIG LOBSTER

Shediac, New Brunswick is on Route 133 around Shediac Bay. It is referred to as the "World's Lobster Capital." Fittingly, in Shediac's Rotary Park sits a giant lobster statue designed by Winston Bronnum. The crushing crustacean weighs fifty-five tonnes with 35 tonnes for its pedestal. The lobster is 35 feet (10.66 metres) long; 16 feet (5 metres) wide; 16 feet (5 metres) high. Bronnum started out by making a paper mache statue of the lobster and the fisherman on it; then he progressed to concrete and steel. Now, *"... the planet's largest crustacean sits ... smiling its lobstery smile for all admirers that travel from around Canada and the world to enjoy (about 500,000 people per year, to be exact!)."*[18]

To boil this lobster, you would need a pot the size of an apartment building.

---

[18] http://www.greatcanadianadventuretour.com/2011/10/worlds-largest-lobster-shediac-new-brunswick/

SUSSEX

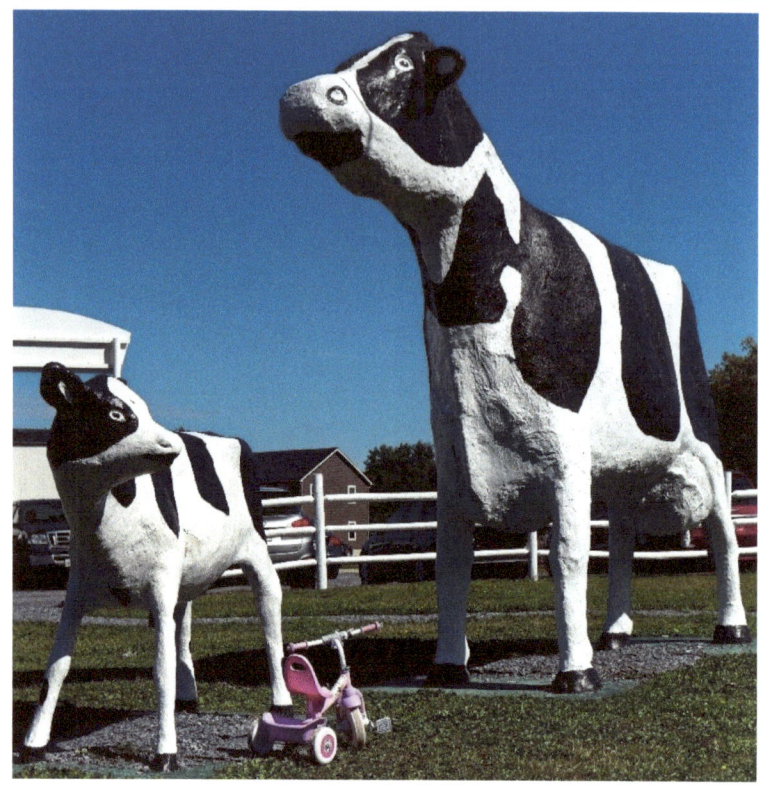

DAISY AND BUTTERCUP

Sussex, New Brunswick is in Kings County and has approximately 4,312 people living there. At the entrance to the town, there are two statues of Holstein cows standing near the Irving Station. Daisy is the mother cow and was built in 1986, while Buttercup (the calf) was erected in 1987. The cow statues are symbolic that Sussex is a major centre for the dairy industry in New Brunswick. The statues are 16 1/2 feet or 5 metres in length and 12 feet or 3.7 metres high.

They are constructed out of cement on wire mesh with welded steel re-bar. Harold MacEachern of Anagance, New Brunswick built Daisy and Buttercup.[19] Near the cow statues, is a potash mine that is permanently closed now, but in the past, its potash was used for fertilizer for the local farms.

---

[19] www.bigthings.ca

NOVA SCOTIA

AULD'S COVE

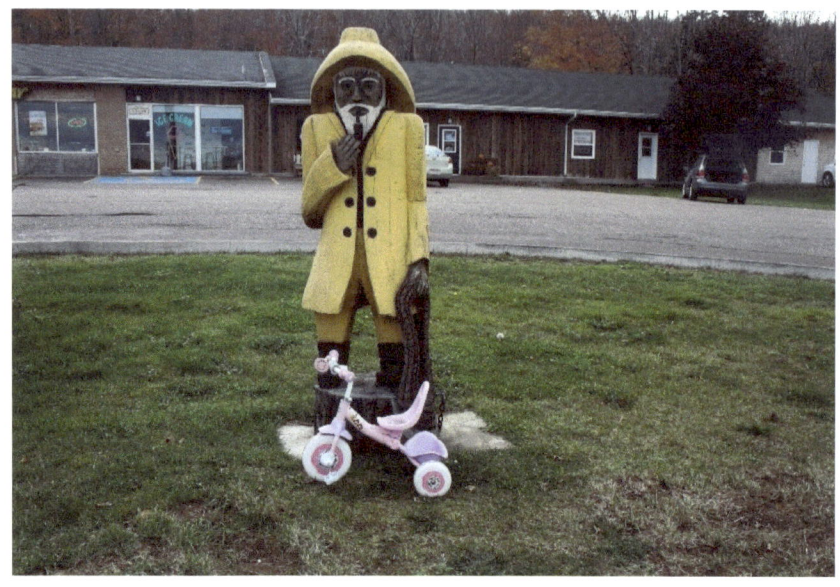

THE MARINER

There is a Mariner statue that can be found in front of the Cove Motel in Auld's Cove. This is just a few minutes away from Cape Breton. The Mariner has some company with him – there is a weathered puffin statue, and an eagle statue as well. Not much information can be found on these statues, but the Mariner is particularly noteworthy for his soulful expression. Auld's Cove is on the western shore of Cabot Strait, opposite to Port Hastings.

BERWICK

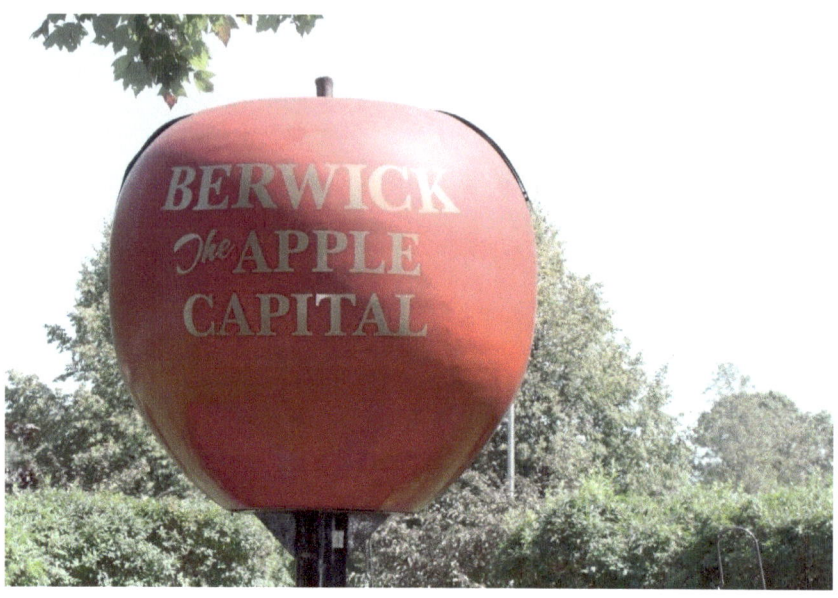

THE BERWICK APPLE

At the town hall, there is a prominent statue of an apple that is symbolic of the economic importance that apple growing has had on the beginnings of Berwick and how its orchards sustain the town today. *"The Berwick area has been a hub for the processing and manufacturing of apple products and the storage and exporting of our famous Nova Scotia quality apples since the early 1900s."*[20] The Berwick apple statue can be found by taking Route 360 and Highway 105.

---

[20] http://www.nsapples.com/applecap.htm

OXFORD

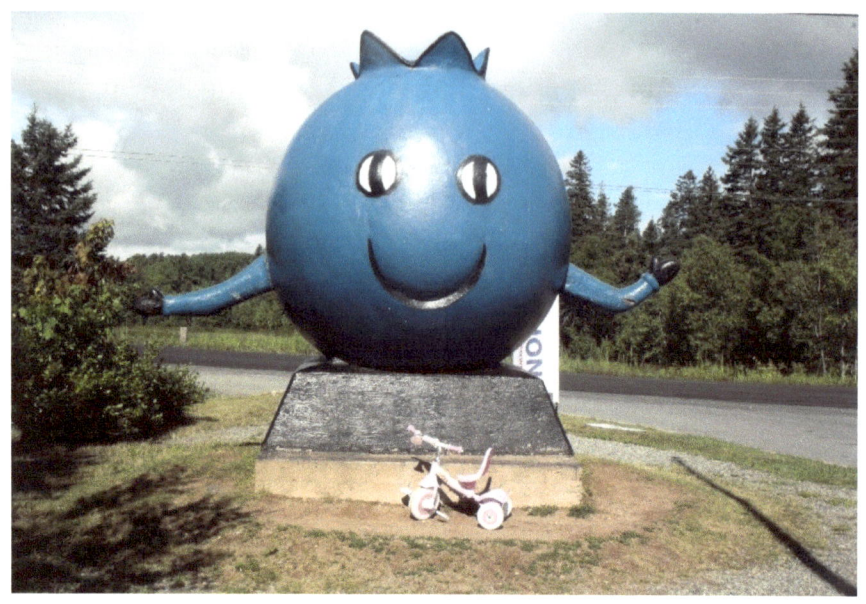

THE GIANT BLUEBERRY

Oxford, Nova Scotia calls itself, "The Blueberry Capital of the World" and has a giant blueberry statue to symbolize it. Apparently, the enormous berry used to be owned by the Mann family of Petitcodiac but Irving Oil bought the humongous blue sphere and brought it to Oxford in 1999. The oversized blueberry is eight feet (2.4 meters) high, ten point eight feet (3.3 meters) wide and weighs eight tonnes.[21]

Ross Rushton, known as, "Wild Blue" has picked blueberries for fifty-five years and comments on the industry: *"I'm only guessing but I feel that 600,000 to 700,000 pounds of blueberries were picked in Nova Scotia back in the 1920s. Today's production is 48-million pounds or more yearly."*[22] Rushton comments that the berries in question are wild blueberries, and feels that they are the best for the world.

---

[21] http://www.bigthings.ca/scotia/oxford.html

[22] http://www.trurodaily.com/Opinion/Columns/2014-08-11/article-3831100/Your-Stories-%26ndash%3B-Local-man-spends-lifetime-in-blueberry-business/1

STEWIACKE

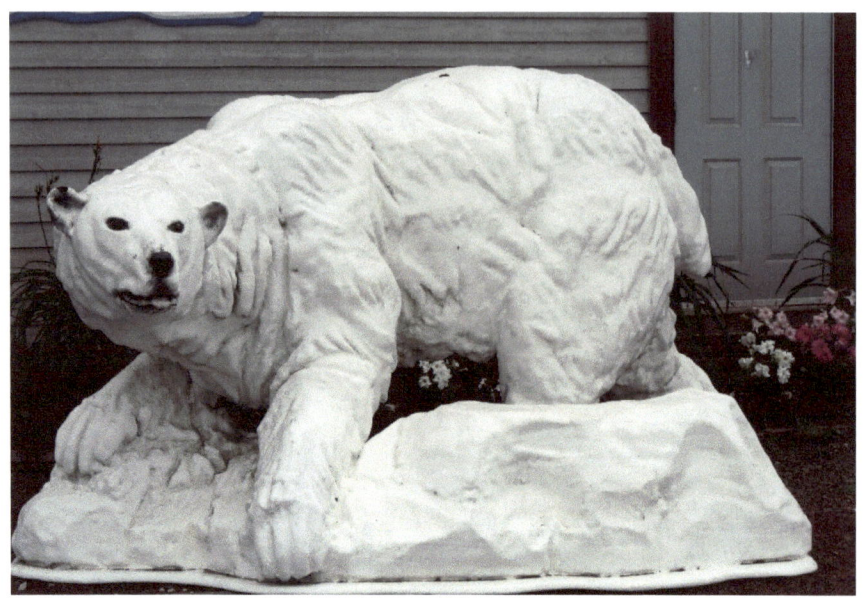

POLAR BEAR

Mastodon Ridge in Stewiacke, Nova Scotia has a statue of a white polar bear. The sign on it says that Stewiacke is located halfway to the Equator, which is 3097 miles away from it. Although the star of the popular tourist site is the Mastodon, the polar bear plays its role too and is considered a mascot. Wikipedia comments:

"The Mastodon Ridge Complex features a craft store, toy store, a mini golf and interpretive centre. Stewiacke is home to two bars, a pharmacy, a grocery store, a pizza store, numerous fast food restaurants, two gas stations, a hardware store, an audio-visual production company, an 18-hole golf course ..."[23]

---

[23] https://en.wikipedia.org/wiki/Stewiacke

ST. PETERS

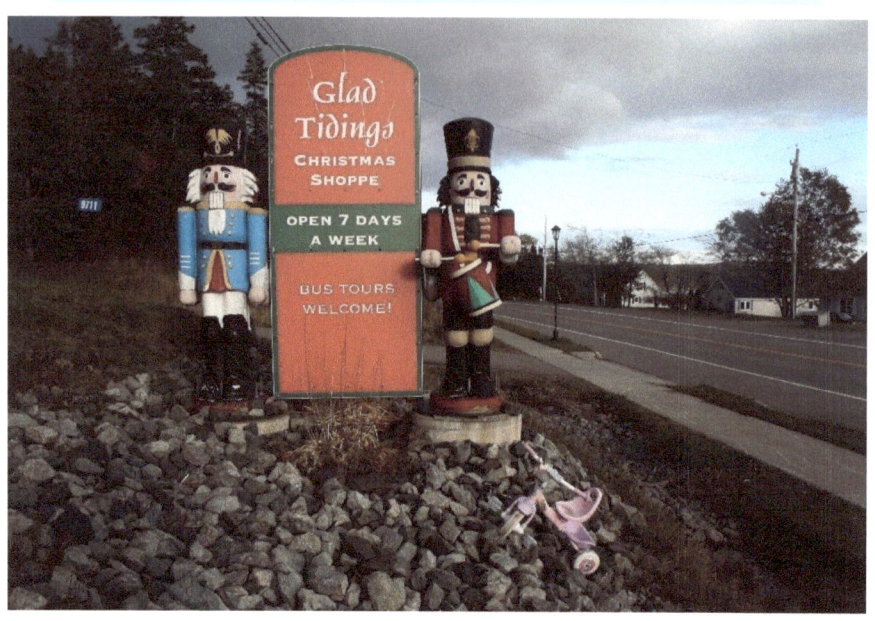

GLAD TIDINGS TOY SOLDIERS

Two toy soldiers stand on each side of the Glad Tidings Christmas Shoppe sign, which can be found at 9711 Grenville Street in St. Peters, Nova Scotia. This is the last year for the shop, but one can only speculate whether-or-not the soldiers will remain or be torn down. The Christmas Shoppe has been in business for the last 24 years, and now it is closing right after Christmas 2016.

TRURO

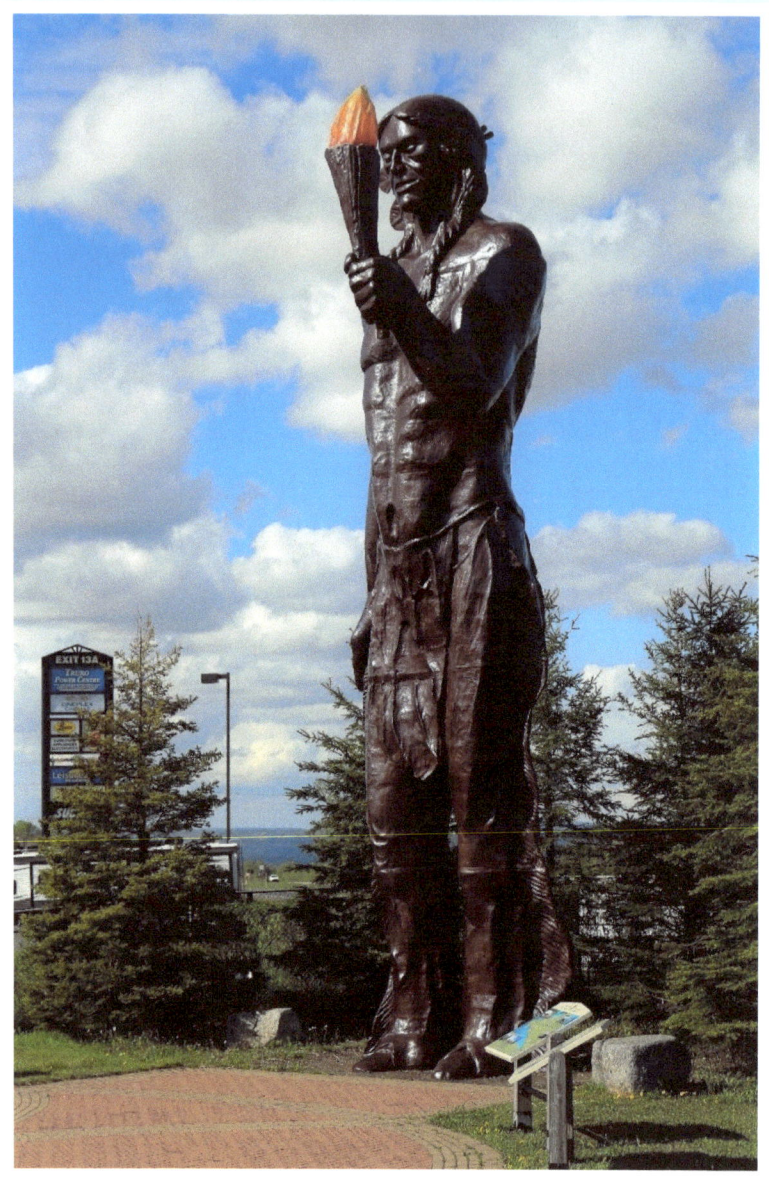

TRURO GLOOSCAP

There on the side of the highway stands a towering statue of "Glooscap." One cannot miss him. Nova Scotia Tourism comments, *"Visit the Glooscap Heritage Centre and Mi'kmaq Museum in Millbrook (Highway 102, Exit 13A) in the Fundy Shore and Annapolis Valley region, which celebrates the area's Mi'kmaq heritage and Glooscap legends. Glooscap, an Abenaki word for "man from nothing" was the first human, created out of a bolt of lightning in the sand, and remains a great figure that appears in many of the Mi'kmaq myths.'*[24]

The interpretation centre which is near the statue of Glooscap presents the history of the Mi'kmaq natives, exhibits the native artifacts, and has a gift shop and tourist information centre.

---

[24] http://www.novascotia.com/see-do/attractions/millbrook-cultural-heritage-centre/1653

WINDSOR

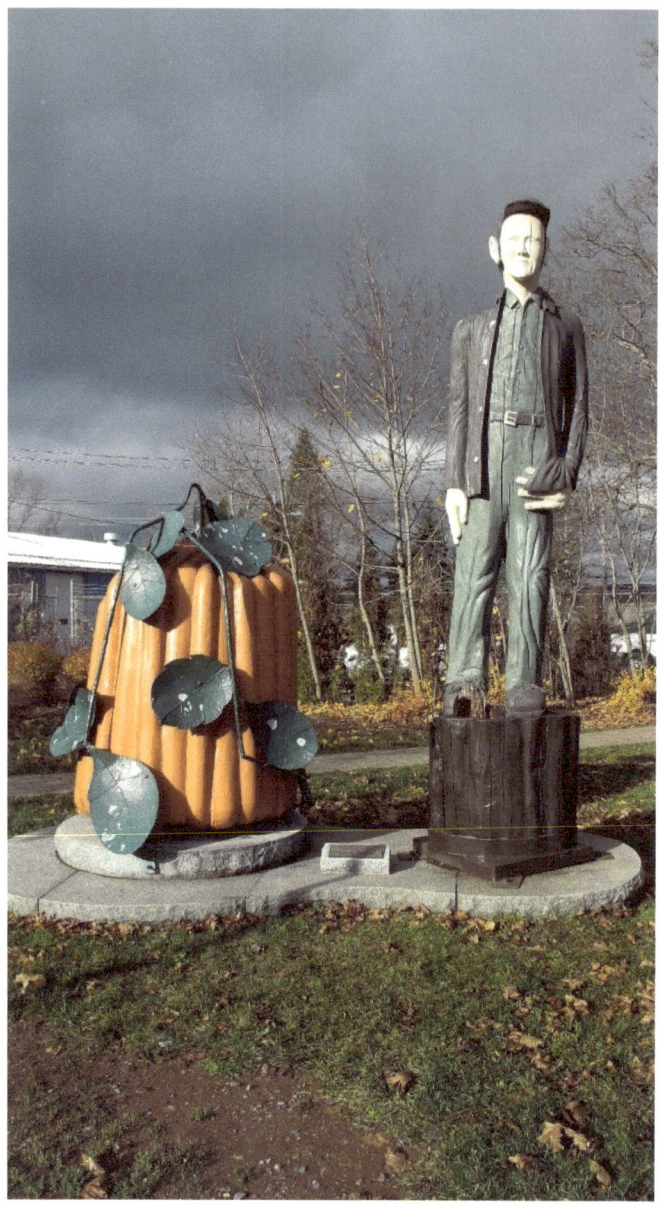

{Photo courtesy of Scott Smith}

THE HOWARD DILL STATUE

Howard Dill invented a special breed of giant pumpkins. Some pumpkins weigh over 1,800 pounds or 800 kilograms. To get to the farm which is now run by Danny Dill, Howard's son, you go to 400 College Road, Windsor, Nova Scotia in the Bay of Fundy, and the Annapolis Valley. Journalist, Julia Scott wrote, "*Twenty-five years ago, a Windsor man named Howard Dill patented a pumpkin seed variety, he named the Atlantic Giant. Dill was a full-time farmer and part-time mad scientist. Home from the evening's chores, he'd work for hours at the kitchen table, doodling pumpkins and taking notes on his experiments...*"[25]

When Dill succeeded in breeding giant pumpkins, he started, "*competitive gardening, allowing men and women around the world to use his seed as the basis for generations of giants that have grown steadily larger each year.*"[26]

Dill died at age 73, in 2008 and is still famous as the Giant Pumpkin King.

---

[25] http://www.juliascott.net/tag/howard-dill/

[26] http://www.wsj.com/articles/SB121279124108553113

PRINCE EDWARD ISLAND

CAVENDISH

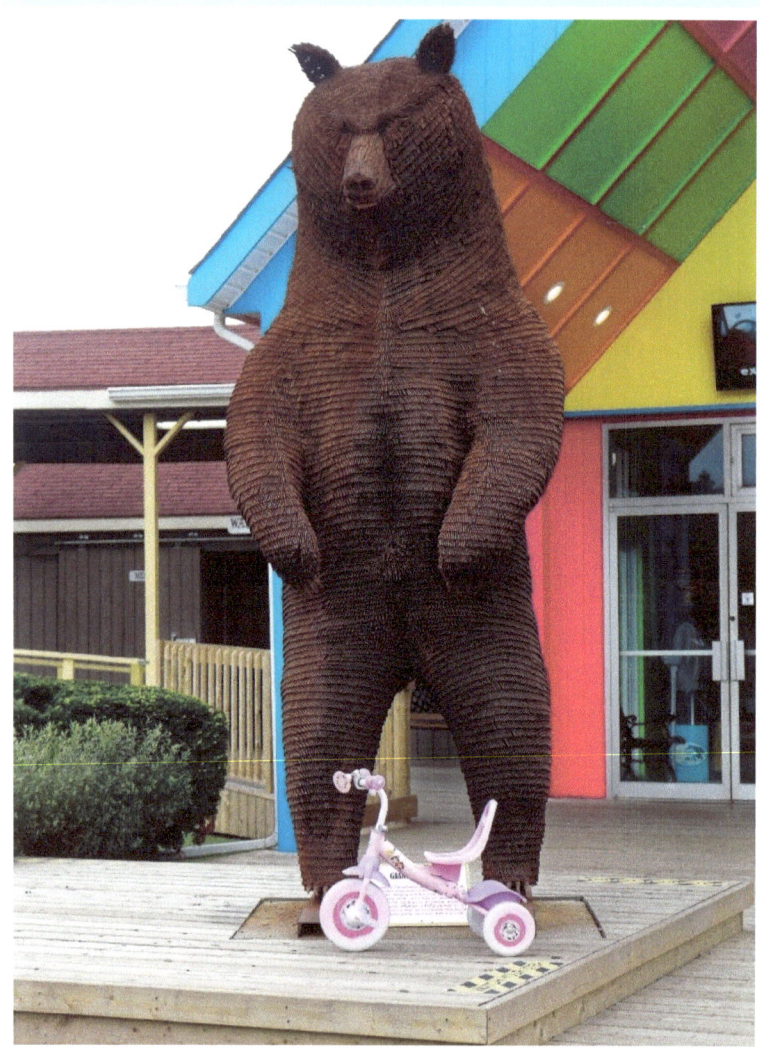

BEAR MADE OF NAILS

At *Ripley's Believe It or Not©* or "Odditorium," in Cavendish, Prince Edward Island; there is a giant bear statue. Bill Secunda of Pennsylvania constructed it. A spokesperson from Ripley's comments, "This life-sized Kodiak grizzly bear is made from over 90,000 common hardware nails -- weighing 3,000 pounds. Secunda is a professional welder and nature lover. He has made numerous other nail art creatures, including a full-sized elk, a bison, and a moose.

The PEI bear statue at Ripley's was acquired from the artist in 2008. It is one of two Secunda bears owned by Ripley's. The other one is on Jeju Island in Korea. In total, Ripley's has 7 large nail animal sculptures by Secunda; all of which are currently on display around the world. In order to find *Ripley's Believe it or Not©*, look for 8863 Cavendish Road, Green Gables, PEI.

CAVENDISH

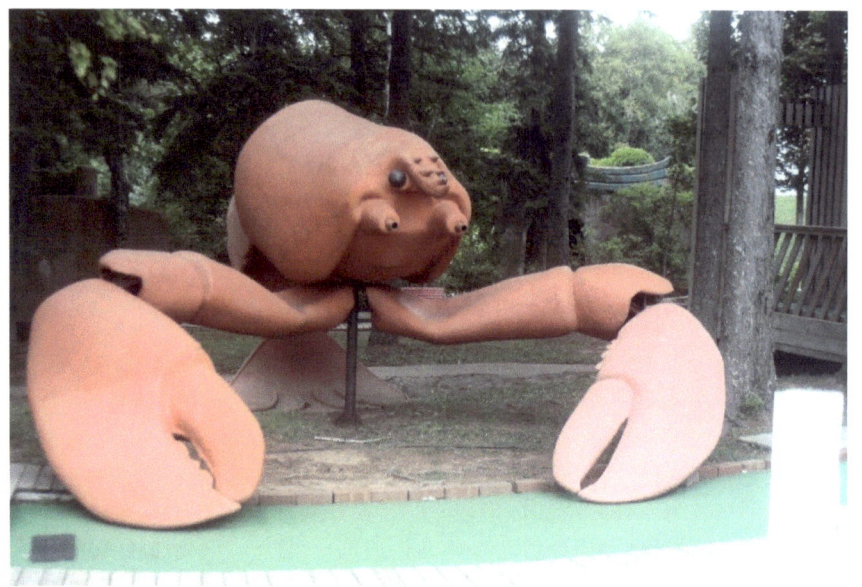

GIANT LOBSTER

A giant, red lobster statue can be found at the River of Adventure Mini Golf course in Cavendish, PEI. There are many challenging hazards in this course, in fact, it is supposed to be impossible to beat. The golf course and lobster have been around for over twenty years. Advertising for the River of Adventure says, *"Putt through the potato patch, play to the top of the Volcano and then over the "Musical" bridge. The course even places you in peril of being eaten by a giant lobster."*[27]

What are the directions to get to the mini golf course? Parks Canada says, *"Follow the signs from the Confederation Bridge (Borden-Carleton, PE) towards Crapaud and Charlottetown (approximately 9.5 km / 6 miles). In Crapaud, turn left onto Route 13. Follow Route 13 until you get to the lights at the junction with Route 6 at Cavendish Corner (approximately 38 km / 23.5 miles)."*[28]

---

[27] http://cavendishsavings.ca/river-of-adventure-mini-golf/
[28] http://www.pc.gc.ca/eng/pn-np/pe/pei-ipe/visit/visit1.aspx

SUMMERSIDE

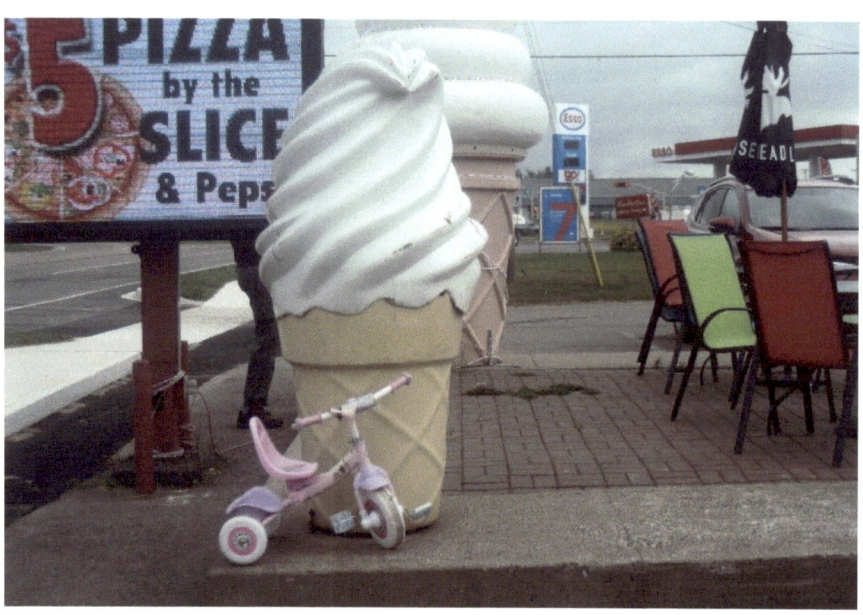

STARLITE ICE CREAM

Driving through Summerside, Prince Edward Island, the traveler will inevitably come across the fifties style, Starlite Diner. It has a huge ice cream cone statue with some smaller ice cream cone statues next to it. Richard Palmer has reopened the diner that he bought from his mother. Not much is known about the ice cream statue, but it stands stalwartly outside the Diner, beckoning the hungry traveler to come in.

Palmer says, "... We're ... going to keep the dairy bar open all year-round. That's a big part of the business, especially in the summer time." He continued, *"... there seems to be a lack of places to eat in Summerside. There are a lot of people who are driving to Charlottetown to go out to dinner. We're hoping to keep more of that crowd in Summerside."* The diner is in a great location and has authentic decor from the fifties. Old gas pumps, jukeboxes, and photos are in the Starlite restaurant and give it its ambiance.

POEM ON BIG STUFF

There are some big statues that we see dotting our land

They are folk art creations that are created, oh, so grand

Some are fish, fowl, caricatures of men or other stuff

Well, we, here in the Maritimes certainly have enough.

New Brunswick has an axe that a giant could swing

And a huge potato who among tubers reigns as king.

In Nova Scotia, there is Glooscap who stands so tall.

And a giant fiddle with a bow which towers over all

Prince Edward Island has cows and lobsters galore

And a statue of Anne of Green Gables on their shore.

The statues often have a story that they are meant to tell

About the lobsters or apples that their region will sell.

Everybody loves things that are made on a colossal scale.

And Maritime statues have a unique and important tale.

ABOUT KATHERINE E. TAPLEY-MILTON

Katherine Tapley-Milton lives with her husband, Dave, and 6 cats in Sackville, New Brunswick. She graduated from Mount Allison University with a B.A. in the areas of psychology, sociology, and history and then got a 2-year Master of Theological Studies degree from Tyndale Seminary in Willowdale, Ontario in 1981. Katherine has been a freelance writer for over 35 years, and her byline has been in hundreds of periodicals.

She also has written, "The Disappearing Mailboxes of New Brunswick and Nova Scotia," in which she has won a Readers' Favorite 5 Star Review Award. Katherine's other books are available online. In May of 2005, she graduated from the BUILT's Customer Service Representative Course in Moncton, N.B. Her hobbies include cooking, organic gardening, writing, reading historical romances, making crafts, and doing volunteer work at the penitentiary.

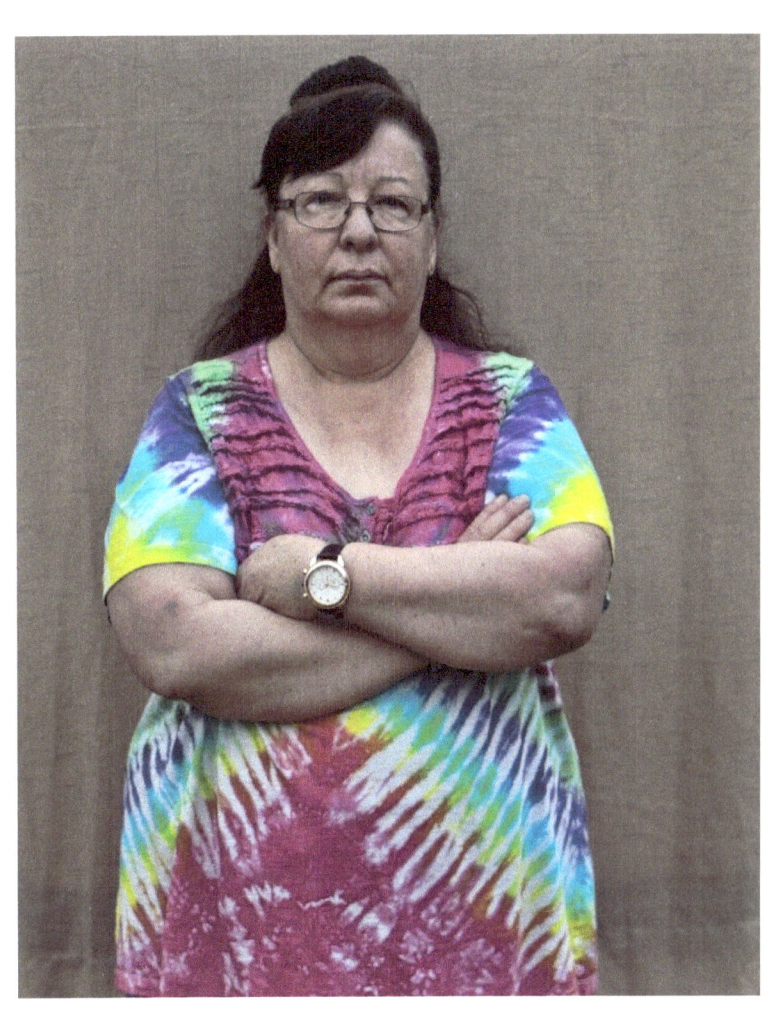

www.ingramcontent.com/pod-product-compliance
Lightning Source LLC
Chambersburg PA
CBHW040235220526
45473CB00001B/250